Who Is Your $ource

Foreword By Bill Vincent

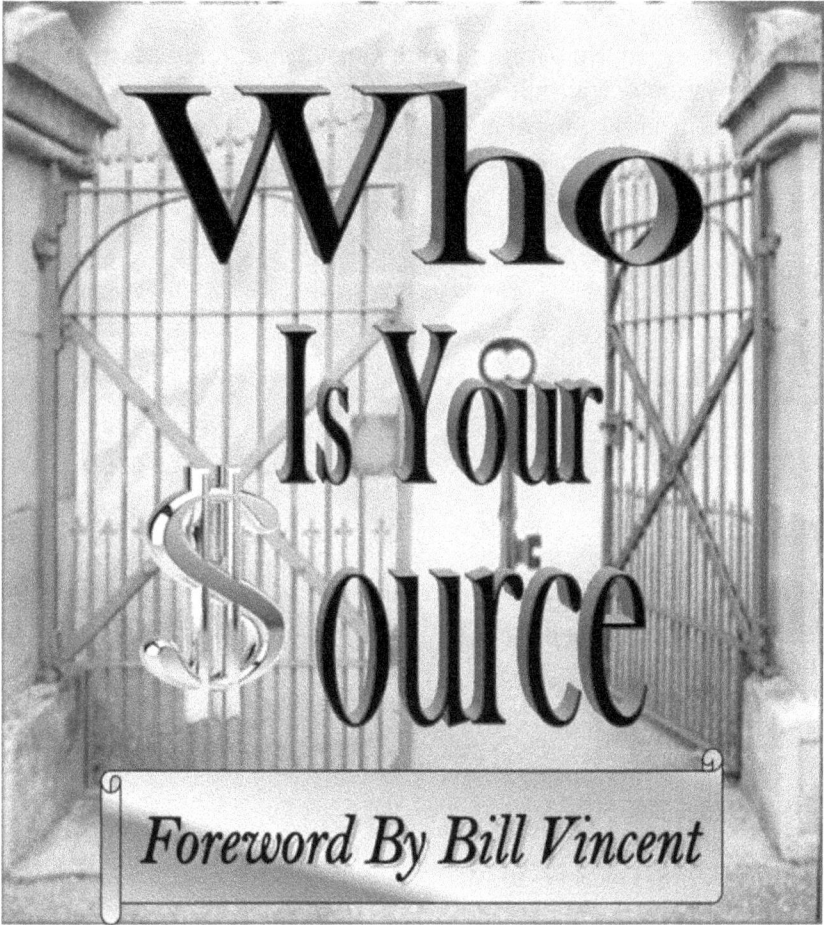

Heaven Or Earth

Kevin Cann

Second Edition

1st Printing

Unless otherwise indicated, all Scripture quotations are taken from *The Holy Bible, New King James Version.* Copyright © 1979, 1980, 1982 by Thomas Nelson, Inc.

LCCN: 2013915524

Ebook 978-1-304-50183-7

Softcover 978-1-62847-563-0

Hardcover 978-1-304-89468-7

PUBLISHED BY REVIVAL WAVES OF GLORY BOOKS & PUBLISHING
www.revivalwavesofglory.com
Litchfield, IL

Printed in the United States of America

Table of Contents

Foreword

Who Is Your Source is an inspiration of powerful truths. I have known Kevin for many years. He is a faithful man of God, and I have been greatly encouraged by his Kingdom insights and revelations over the years. He is literally humble servant of God with a passion to see the Kingdom of God manifest.

Kevin is a fresh breath of God's divine order when it comes to finances. Kevin truly understands God's principles on earth as it is in Heaven. In this cutting edge book, Kevin reveals many truths through many of his personal experiences. This book will stir a response that can at times be uncomfortable but is necessary. Prepare yourself to be touched by God through *Who Is Your Source*. This world is consumed by having their needs met more than God's Kingdom System being established. I am convinced the truths in this book will set many free and will be used to change the lives of millions. Kevin's book will draw you closer to God and will help unlock many of the mysteries of the Kingdom of God.

Bill Vincent

Revival Waves of Glory Ministries

Solid Reasons Why Kingdom Principles Work Review

It doesn't take long to reflect on the fact that we are living in very uncertain times. Author Kevin Cann has a strong message for us in this time and that is for us to consider who our true foundation needs to be anchored in.

He very carefully lays out for us the 2 vastly different kingdoms- God's kingdom and Satan's- and then shares how many of the worldly systems operate. You will be refreshed with solid Biblical principles that will verify God's way of success. The fallacies of the financial system in offering those in debt loans keeps individuals a slave to the system while in essence shuts down one's chances of fulfilling their destiny. Cann believes many look to unions as their source of job protection. A man made system, he believes, will always keep you in bondage to itself.

Even in Christian circles, if one is manipulated in the religious system they are taught to give so that they can get something. God loves a cheerful giver and you will be shown how, in the sowing and reaping principle that you cannot out give God.

The welfare system has made individuals dependent on it and, with all their needs met, many have no desire to seek work. Contrasting that with the kingdom system, we first must sow into our work before God gives us a harvest. As our hearts are extended toward others and we wait on God's timing, we are positioned for due blessings.

Whether it is business, personal, or family decisions, allowing God to be the source of wisdom will prove beneficial. Learn more in depth reasons as to why following the kingdom system over the world's system is the way to go. As you do you will recognize more who truly is your source.

By **Valerie Caraotta**

Dedication

I would like to dedicate this book to my Heavenly Father. He gave me the words to put in this book. This book would not be possible without the help of the Holy Spirit giving me guidance and direction. I am thankful to Jesus Christ for saving me from my sins. I thank all three from the bottom of my heart.

Introduction

I am writing this book to explain who the true source is through good or bad times. God is your source no matter what the situation may be in your life.

Over the past three and a half to four years, the United States and the rest of the world has been in an economic crisis. Banks have failed, governments have failed, and businesses have closed. People have lost jobs and faith in entities they thought were their source. These are the times when God reveals Himself as the only true source for everything we need or want. Philippians 4:19 "And my God shall supply all your need according to His riches in Glory by Christ Jesus." Psalm 37:4 "Delight yourself also in the Lord; And He shall give you the desires of your heart."

We always want to put our trust in people or things that can't provide a true source. We think our job is our source. Some people believe the government is their source. While others believe money is their source. But as the past crisis has revealed, all of these sources are vulnerable. My God is not vulnerable to anything in this world, because He is the Creator/Owner of it all. Revelation 4:11b "For You created all things, And by Your will they exist and were created."

I was in a prophetic meeting last night and I noticed something very interesting that I would like to share with everyone. Usually at the end of a service, an offering is taken up for the prophet. Those who support the prophet of God will receive a reward/blessing because they are receiving God's representative. Here is what I noticed in this meeting and many other meetings as well: the people see and hear the prophetic gift in action but when it comes time to give to the prophet, people get up and leave. I was not there to get a word from the prophet. I was there to sow into the prophet because God has shown me the power of sowing into the prophetic anointing. I believe we are sowing into our future because the prophet sees and hears in the future. This is the reason I was there. I wanted to sow my seed into the prophetic because there is a special anointing that takes your seed and multiplies it. Matthew 10:41a "He who receives a prophet in the name of a prophet shall receive a prophet's reward." Many people just want a word from the prophet and do not sow into him. When you don't sow into the prophet, you are not receiving the prophet, therefore, God can't give you a prophet's reward. Most people are going because they want a word from God, to help them in their situation. The answer to our situations is not in the prophetic word. God will send us the answer when we sow into the prophetic. He is waiting on us, so He can move on our behalf. He wants something from us and instead we are trying to get something from Him. If we will change our point of view when we enter a prophetic meeting, we will be blessed and His prophets will be blessed as well.

I am writing this after the 2012 Presidential election. I did notice that voters were voting with their wallets. What I mean is that voters that rely on the government as their source came out and voted accordingly. This is just another example of people putting their trust in man instead of God. I have another point to add to this as well. During Thanksgiving a movie was released about Lincoln. In this movie, Lincoln and the government were actually fighting to free the slaves. Today the opposite is true. The government would like to enslave people with their social programs and replace God in their lives as their source. The end result is that people must choose God as their only true source.

CHAPTER 1
World Systems-
Personal

There are two systems on this earth. The first is God's system/Kingdom system. The reason God's system existed on this earth before Satan's is because God created the earth. That means He created the one true Kingdom system in the beginning. The second system is Satan's system/man's system. His system is a counterfeit to God's system because he cannot create anything, only copy what God has created. These are two very different systems that are opposite of each other. All manmade systems have similar characteristics because the soul is in charge of these systems. Control and deception are the biggest characteristics. Greed and manipulation are also a huge part of manmade systems. Man's system can be found from the time we are born until we die. When we are first introduced into this world, the first thing we encounter is the manmade systems. We are all born in a hospital that is part of the healthcare system. When we are born, the only thing we know is that someone takes care of us and supplies everything we need: food, shelter, etc. We have no idea where it comes from. At the end of our life, we encounter the manmade system too. We all have to die at some point and the government and healthcare system is there at the end of our lives, as well.

Marriage System

In today's society the marriage system is being distorted. It is based on the feelings and emotions of individuals. If it "feels good" we do it. Today marriage is not taken seriously. We live together, in order to see if it will work out before we get married. The government system encourages this action with their tax laws. It is more profitable to live together and not be married, than to live together and be married. Man has even corrupted this system by trying to convince us that two women or two men together is a marriage. The difference between the marriage system and all the other systems that I will discuss in this book is that God did create marriage.

Satan is just trying to destroy the very foundation of society by destroying the marriage bond. Marriage is a sacred bond between a woman and a man. This bond or commitment is put together by God. He is the creator of marriage. So He would know the right people to put together in a marriage. My wife and I were put together by God. We knew within a few weeks of dating that we were the one for each other. We were married five months after we met. She spent three of those months planning the wedding. So often we think we know what is best for us. Many people try to play God and choose their own spouse. Sometimes other people try to play match maker. My wife and I did have a mutual friend that introduced us to each other. She was instrumental in helping us communicate with each other, but God was using her to accomplish His plan. My wife and I both knew this marriage was from God. We are just beginning to know each other. We have adjustments to make but we always remember that God put us together. If this marriage was up to us, we would not have married each other. We knew God was the source of this marriage. So often we don't look to God as our source for everything. I believe this is one reason the church doesn't look any different than the world does, in this regard. In the church there is a high rate of divorce that is no different than the world's high rate. God needs to be our source for everything and that includes our relationships. In Genesis 2:24 "Therefore a man shall leave his father and mother and be joined to his wife, and they shall become one flesh." In Hebrews 13:4 "Marriage is honorable to all, and the bed undefiled; but fornicators and adulterers God will judge."

Education System

We are taught this manmade system in our education system. I have a financial degree from Texas Tech University. I don't want people to think my school or our education system is bad, but it is a manmade system. We are taught that we need a degree to get a job, buy a house and save for retirement. That is the selling point for higher education. The problem I have with this concept is higher education doesn't teach you a skill or any real world experience. It's all theory based from the manmade system. The only thing higher education teaches is the concept of the manmade system.

And let me say this, higher education is definitely in it for the money. This is what keeps the system going. Just think about this for a moment: we get loans to go to school so we can get better jobs so we can buy better things and live in a nicer house. So we go into debt, because the system says we need higher education to make a good living. Then we get out of school and can't find a job because we have no experience or skill, but still have to make the loan payments. This is job security for the people who teach higher education. So you see, I have been in this manmade system and experienced what it has to offer. I can honestly say that someone can learn just as much, if not more, by reading lots of books and getting personal experience. The system says that we need a degree to get a job, so now everyone has degrees. Next the system says we need to get a master's degree because that will separate us from everyone with a bachelor's degree. You see it never ends and that is why I believe in real world experience over higher education. Knowledge is power. 1 Samuel 2:3 "Talk no more so very proudly; let no arrogance come from your mouth, For the Lord is the God of knowledge; and by Him actions are weighed."

Financial System

The financial system is based upon what man thinks it should be. When the "recession" came it was because the manmade system got too greedy. Everyone in the system got too greedy, not just Wall Street. This of course proves that a manmade system is not perfect. There will always be problems with a manmade system. The financial system in this world is not intended to help everyone. For example, if you are a person who only uses cash to purchase items, then you have no credit built up. According to the manmade system, credit is what you need to borrow money from a bank or get a credit card. Now let's talk about what debt does to someone. Debt is man's system of being able to afford things you don't need but want. You actually are penalized if you have no credit, even if you have paid cash for everything you possess. Your credit score could actually be lower if you have no debt out there. This makes no sense because the objective is to get everyone to adhere to the manmade system.

Once everyone does that, then the system has control over your life. The system knows how undisciplined the average person can become with their money. I will give a basic example of the system in action. Let's say someone buys a house, car or whatever, and they get in over their head in debt. The person can file for bankruptcy and before the ink is dry on the paper work, they are receiving offers in the mail for credit cards, car loans, etc. Now the banks made money while the person was paying the payments and probably sold the house or car and received something. The bankruptcy lawyer made some good money off of the process, as well. So why would the system send someone loan applications who just defaulted on their previous loans? The objective of the system is to keep you coming back for more and make you the slave to the system. It's really a modern day slavery operation, if you really look at it from the outside. Under this system, we stay in a servitude type of mind set. Satan's goal is to keep us in this system so that we will not fulfill our destiny. I'm speaking from personal experience. As I write this book, I'm in a large amount of credit card debt that makes me have to go to work every day to keep making the payments. Until I pay them off, I will not be free from this servitude. I just got married recently, so we had two incomes coming in instead of one. I thought this would help pay down the debt, but my wife lost her job. So now I'm supporting two people instead of one, plus the debt.

The reason I share this with you is because you never know what could happen next. If I had minimal debt this would be no problem with a loss of income, but now it is compounded even more, because of the debt. Now I didn't wake up one day and this all happened at once.

This occurred over time. I will go back and explain the process of getting to this place. I made an investment that was from God. I purchased some Ford stock, but because I didn't have any cash, I used credit cards to buy the stock. This is not a bad idea as long as the cards get paid off from the proceeds. So I purchased the stock and it went up and I sold the stock for a good profit. My problem was, I didn't take the amount I had invested to pay off the credit cards. So now I'm left with credit card debt. You may ask what I did with the money I made from the stock. I bought a new computer system for my office. I could have done without that.

I also bought a used BMW car. It was the first nice car I had ever bought. I did pay cash for it, but I should have paid off my credit cards first. So you see, now I'm burning through the cash and I still have the debt out there. So to someone on the outside, it might look like I'm doing really well. This is my point here: That is part of the manmade system. If I was doing really well, I wouldn't have to go to work every day. It's very easy to get caught up in the manmade system. Now each individual has to be responsible for their own actions, but society as a whole does not teach discipline in the debt area. Society actually fuels the system by using media and marketing. We are bombarded with ads of everything, every day, on all media outlets. Proverbs 22:7 "The rich rule over the poor, and the borrower is servant to the lender."

Organized Labor

Another man made system I would like to discuss is organized labor. Now I believe when unions were formed, there was a need for them to protect the worker from harmful situations. Today, unions are just another manmade system that says you need to pay dues and we will get you a job and keep your job and protect you from the company. We will negotiate your contract for you. The union is basically saying, "Pay us to take care of you". The union member is looking for some type of security. When someone enters this type of agreement, they are saying that the union is now their source. The union is their god and the union controls the members. Therefore, whatever the union leaders believe is what they instill in the members. In effect the member becomes enslaved to the union. This is no different than being enslaved to debt or some other manmade system. The belief is that everyone in a union is working together but in the end it's all about the individual. At the true heart of organized labor is selfishness. It's all about "me". During the time when automotive companies had to close plants and lay off thousands of workers, who lost out? The members lost their jobs but the union just lost some dues. Now who is still getting paid? The leaders are still getting paid. If I was a union member and this happened to me, I would not support them in the future.

But members will still do it because of their belief in organized labor as their source. Another example is Hostess. The company went bankrupt, thousands lost jobs but union leaders still get their paycheck.

My point is that these members have looked to the union as their source. The union, just like all manmade systems, failed them. We cannot look to man as our source. Man has been trying to copy God's system since the beginning of time. The problem with society is that no one wants to take responsibility for anything. It's easier to let someone else do it for them. What they don't realize is that this comes at a cost. You give up control of your life to that person or system. This is why most union members have the same perception of certain things in life. For instance: most union members vote for the same political party. The belief that the union leaders instill into the members: if you vote for a political party, the system will keep working for everyone. When this happens, every member is giving up more and more of their life to the manmade system. This system will eventually fail them. If we take a look at society today, we can see that we are not better off because of these manmade systems. It all comes down to personal responsibility.

Today in our society, no one wants to take responsibility for anything. That is why the manmade systems are growing. It's easier to let someone else do it for us. It's too much work to have to take personal responsibility for our actions. We live in a microwave society that wants everything now. We are giving up more of our own freedom and the manmade system is becoming more powerful every day. James 3:14-16 "But if you have bitter envy and self-seeking in your hearts, do not boast and lie against the truth. This wisdom does not descend from above, but is earthly, sensual, and demonic. For where envy and self-seeking exist, confusion and every evil thing are there."

Favoritism System

Another man made system is favoritism. First, workers are subject to do whatever the master/boss wants. Second is that they are tied down to their job. In fact they are giving up future opportunities just to stay in the favoritism system. Oh sure, they might get a promotion here or there but is that really their full potential? You see, a manmade system will always keep you in bondage to itself and never let you experience the full potential that God has for you on this earth. The idea of any manmade system is to take the freedom you have within, so that the destiny God has planned for you will not prevail. All manmade systems have a false sense of security with them, that, from the outside looks great. But once inside the system, it becomes a deception that many people cannot get out of.

Proverbs 12:2 "A good man obtains favor from the Lord, but a man of wicked intentions He will condemn." Colossians 3:23 "And whatever you do, do it heartily, as to the Lord and not to men, knowing that from the Lord you will receive the reward of inheritance; for you serve the Lord Christ." Proverbs 28:23 "He who rebukes a man will find more favor afterward than he who flatters with the tongue."

Religious System

Now let's talk about my favorite manmade system: religion. Yes that's right, religion is a manmade system.

It's probably one of the oldest manmade systems. Most people think of religion as Catholic, Baptist, Presbyterian, etc. These are just different forms of religion. In religion, the manmade system is in control of you and your finances. That means, we are doing what the system wants instead of what God wants us to do with His resources. The church controls people by implying they must give in the offering or something will happen to them. Fear is a powerful tool in religion. No man should tell us to give to anything. This must come from God. Everyone should give their tithe to their church. Also, another common manmade gesture is to give when you need something from God. This is like trying to buy a miracle. In other words, a preacher might say," If you need a new car, house or healing in your body, give a thousand dollar offering right now." I have been in services where this happens and I have given an offering of a thousand dollars, but only because God told me to give it, not some man. This leads into control and manipulation of people. God doesn't need our money. He is looking at our heart. The amount doesn't matter to God, unless He gives you a certain amount to give and you don't do it.

The manmade system wants to control the flow of resources. If man can do this then he has you. The church will even preach that if you don't give you will go to hell. This is just a scare tactic. Another religious mind set is that having money is evil. God never said that having money is evil, but that the **love** of money is evil. 1 Timothy 6:10 "For the love of money is a root of all kinds of evil, for which some have strayed from the faith in their greediness, and pierced themselves through with many sorrows." That means if you love money, getting money, working to make money, more than loving God, its evil.

The church wants us to believe that we are not supposed to have money. This concept is based on the idea that remaining poor is a humbling experience. Jesus and His Disciples were not poor. I am supposed to follow His example. The religious minds have interpreted this to their advantage. That is a false teaching that the religious leaders would want you to believe so they can be in control of the manmade system. There is nothing wrong with being humble. I remind myself all the time no matter how much money I have it's not mine to begin with; I'm a manager of God's resources.

Another false doctrine that the religious church teaches is that we are getting out of here soon because Jesus is coming back. They will teach that there is no hope, future or destiny. This is using fear to manipulate people. And let me tell you, they make a lot of money promoting this doom and gloom mind set. Selling teachings on cd, DVD and books is one way to make money from fear. Also by having conferences and charging people that attend. They are selling fear and a lot of people are buying it. Just like when leaders will tell people to stock up on food and other things because the end of the world is coming soon. We are supposed to occupy the earth until Jesus comes back, not give the world up. That is the reason there is worldly people occupying the seven mountains instead of believers. The seven mountains in society are; media, government, education, economy, religion, arts, and family. God is coming back for a glorious Church. James 1:26-27 "If anyone among you thinks he is religious, and does not bridle his tongue but deceives his own heart, this one's religion is useless. Pure and undefiled religion before God and the Father is this; to visit orphans and widows in trouble, and to keep oneself unspotted from the world."

CHAPTER 2
World Systems-Government

Judicial System

A lawsuit is another great example. The first thought that enters someone's mind when they feel they have been wronged, is to sue that person or business. I'll give you a personal example of this; I was terminated at my former job. My co-worker committed the same act as I did but only received a written warning. I could go to a lawyer and have him try to sue the company for wrongful termination. I don't want to do that because God is my source not the company. Now how did we get to be a society that takes no personal responsibility for our own actions? Manmade system is: we sue, we get money, lawyer gets his cut, the person or entity has insurance and everyone is happy. The problem with this outlook on life is that everyone in society pays for that lawsuit, one way or another. Let me explain, if the insurance has to pay a claim for a lawsuit or you wrecking your car, where does the money come from? Most people think: *well, I have been paying in for years, so they already have the money.*

That's true, but insurance companies don't take losses. They will increase the rates for everyone to recoup their money in a lawsuit. That means everyone in society pays for a lawsuit. That brings me back to personal responsibility: if everyone would be responsible for their own problems and not blame other people or entities for their problems, we would live in a much better world. So, society would rather shift the blame to someone else. Now there are some situations that are of no fault to the victim. They should be compensated. Where there is money to be made, however, people get greedy. The greed is what empowers the manmade system. Then it starts to affect our political system, too. I live in Madison County, IL. It is considered a "judicial hellhole" because of the very reasons I have discussed.

The county and some of the people who live in it, not all by the way, have created a very profitable manmade system. Many frivolous lawsuits have been won in this county. Now the county is run by trial lawyers and all the money they have won. Most businesses don't want to come here anymore. It affects all aspects of society.

It affects the everyday worker, the businessman, and the average family. We all have less because a small group of people want more. I don't have a problem with someone wanting more, but there is a right way and a wrong way to achieve that goal. Manmade systems are self-centered and selfish. It's all about "me". They don't care who they hurt or how they get there. Deception is a powerful tool of the manmade system. People believe that they are doing right, when in reality they are not. It's also very difficult to convince someone that they are deceived. Usually the only way for someone to break free of deception is for them to see the error of their ways on their own. God can open their eyes and then they can see the light, but trying to get someone to see the light on their own is very difficult. 1 Corinthians 6:5-6 "I say this to your shame. Is it so, that there is not a wise man among you, not even one, who will be able to judge between his brethren? But brother goes to law against brother and that before believers!" In Luke 11:39 "Then the Lord said to him, "Now you Pharisees make the outside of the cup and dish clean, but your inward part is full of greed and wickedness." Proverbs 25:8-10

"Do not go hastily to court; for what will you do in the end, when your neighbor has put you to shame? Debate your case with your neighbor, and do not disclose the secret to another; lest he who hears it expose your shame, and your reputation be ruined."

Criminal System

This system is definitely a manmade system. I will give you a personal experience about this system. My brother and I were working on a truck at my parents company one day. We were trying to "pop start" the truck which a neighbor had mistaken as possible gun fire.

They called the police and several police cars came with guns drawn on us. We tried to explain who we were but the police did not want to listen. In the end my brother and I got roughed up by the police for being on our own property and trying to start a truck. The problem with this manmade system is that some police want to treat everyone as a criminal first. The part that bothers me is the police get away with this a lot. They are supposed to serve and protect us, the taxpayers of this state. The taxpayers are the ones who pay the police officers' salaries. Another point I would like to make is this system is just like all the other systems because they are in it for the money. In Illinois where I live, it is denied by most, but everyone knows they have a ticket quota for each month. That is not what this system was designed to do. It was designed to enforce the law. Once again man has corrupted a system to their benefit. In Galatians 6:7-8 "Do not be deceived, God is not mocked; whatever a man sows, that he will also reap. For he who sows to his flesh will of the flesh reap corruption, but he who sows to the Spirit will of the Spirit reap everlasting life"

Welfare System

The next system I would like to discuss is the welfare system. This too is a manmade system that puts people in bondage to the government. Then, guess what happens: the government is now their source. Now just like all manmade systems it tries to copy God's system. The government is willing to take care of you, but it will cost you something. The cost is control of your life. This is the modern day version of slavery. If you look back to the slave days, the slave relied on the master for all of his needs. This would include shelter, food, clothing, and health care. The master was the slave's source. Fast forward to 2013 and we will see not too much has changed; it's just in a more modern form. In 2013 there are more people on welfare in America than ever before in history. The definition of master: one who has control over another or others. The definition of a slave: one bound in servitude as the property of a person or household. We have generations who are growing up on this manmade system. Just like in the slavery days, these generations believe this is a normal way of life.

There is nothing normal about giving up control of your life and being in bondage to a master. God created us to be free. Sure there has been an economic crisis, but that just proves that the manmade systems don't work. In order to fix one system that failed, the government is using this opportunity to expand another system, which will fail eventually. All manmade systems fail at some point in time because they are made by man and he is not perfect. God is perfect and that is why His systems work all the time, no matter the circumstances.

There is no incentive to get off food stamps (SNAP). The system encourages people to keep using it. If you don't have to work and you have food in the fridge, why would you go look for work? The longer people stay on the system the harder it is for them to get off and the more control they give up. Once the system has them, then the recipients must follow the system rules. This is where an individual begins to compromise their freedom. Once the system becomes their source, the recipient/slave will do whatever the master wants to keep the benefits coming to them.

An example of this would be to vote for a political party because that party supports this social program. The recipient is now in bondage to the master. During the writing of this book my wife and I both lost our jobs. We both tried to get unemployment and were denied. We are not receiving any type of government assistance at all. In Illinois, where I worked, that does not happen very often. The government usually rules in favor of the employee, not the employer. I believe this denial is part of God's plan for Him to be our only true source. We are truly living this book in real life. In Proverbs 6:9-11 "How long will you slumber, O sluggard? When will you rise from your sleep? A little sleep, a little slumber, a little folding of the hands to sleep- So shall your poverty come on you like a prowler, and your need like an armed man." Also in Proverbs 10:4 "He who has a slack hand becomes poor, but the hand of the diligent make rich." In Proverbs 12:24 "The hand of the diligent will rule, but the lazy man will be put to forced labor." In Proverbs 14:23 "In all labor there is profit, but idle chatter leads only to poverty." In Proverbs 19:24 "A lazy man buries his hand in the bowl, and will not so much as bring it to his mouth."

Also in Proverbs 20:4 "The lazy man will not plow in winter; he will beg during harvest and have nothing." Proverbs 26:13-16 "The lazy man says, "there is a lion in the road! A fierce lion is in the streets!" As a door turns on its hinges, so does the lazy man on his bed. The lazy man buries his hand in the bowl; it wearies him to bring it back to his mouth. The lazy man is wiser in his own eyes than seven men who can answer sensibly."

Healthcare System

The healthcare system can be an extension of the welfare system. We rely on the government to supply our healthcare needs. Most people look to doctors and medicine to fix our problems. I do believe that God uses doctors and medicine to heal people. However, we should look to God as our source of healing. The problem I have encountered is that people look to the manmade system first and then when that doesn't work they will come to God. He is to be our source for everything. If we go to Him and He guides us down a path that leads to a surgery or some type of medicine then that is the right path. We almost always want a quick fix to our problem. Most medicines only treat the symptoms but God heals it from the root. That is the reason so many people are on medicines today that they do not need to be taking. The system works like this; we feel a pain, then go to the doctor, he or she says you have this or that and you need to take these pills to make it go away. The doctor makes money off the visit, and then the pharmacy makes money selling you the pills. Then the pharmaceutical company makes money making the pills. We pay health insurance for all of this and the insurance company makes money off of that. We need to look to God as our source of healing and prosperity in health. Isaiah 53:5 "But He was wounded for our transgressions, He was bruised for our iniquities; the chastisement for our peace was upon Him, and by His stripes we are healed." In Acts 9:34 "And Peter said to him, "Aeneas, Jesus Christ heals you. Arise and make your bed." Then he arose immediately." In 3 John 1:2 "Beloved, I pray that you may prosper in all things and be in health, just as your soul prospers."

Political System

When this country was founded and the Constitution was written, the people involved in that process knew that this country should have a foundation built upon God. The founding fathers of this country knew that God was the true source of our government. The political process should be by the people and for the people. It has turned into some kind of elite club. We have an elite club making decisions about the people's health care benefits that they themselves do not use. The politicians have the best health care and do not pay anything for it. How do they know what is best for us? Also they can invest in stocks and other investments that would be considered "conflict of interest" to the rest of us. You see over the years politicians have created a manmade system that benefits them. That is the problem with a manmade system; it can start out with good intentions but man always seems to find a way to corrupt it. The reason for that is because man is born into a fallen world. So man uses his soul to make decisions instead of his spirit. World systems are built from the foundations of the soul. Isaiah 9:6 "for unto us a Child is born, unto us a Son is given; and the government will be upon His shoulder. And His name will be called Wonderful,

Counselor, Mighty God, Everlasting Father, Prince of Peace."

CHAPTER 3
World Systems-
Business

Venture Capital System

The next system I would like to discuss is venture capital. I first would like to say that I have a finance degree and do not believe all venture capital is bad. Just like I don't believe all debt is bad. The system of venture capital is made by man, so it is flawed. Since most people know about Facebook, this is the easiest example out there. Everyone looks at all the money the creator of Facebook is worth, but nobody realizes how much he gave up to get there and also how much other people made too. The problem I see with venture capital is this; when someone is trying to get capital for their idea, the creator gives up way too much to get the capital. It's as though you are signing your life away to the venture capitalists. Basically this is how it goes: creator comes up with idea, goes to VC for money, gets money but gives up half of company or more, now VC tells creator of idea what to do to get it to market, so VC can cash out and do it all over again. Now, I'm an investor just like the VC and I understand the risks they take and that a lot of investments fail. I also understand that investors should be rewarded for their risk. I am talking about the actual system that the VC's have created which benefits themselves. Once an entrepreneur gets inside that system they are giving up freedoms, just like all the other manmade systems I have discussed earlier. This is real hard to see for most people, because the average person doesn't know how this works. I have an inside view because I'm an investor. The problem is that most of the successful VC's have a lot of money, power, and influence. This becomes a great marketing tool to the entrepreneur. I believe it's best to "bootstrap" a startup idea for as long as possible. Bootstrap is just using the cash you have and not spending money on any unnecessary things.

This will put the entrepreneur in better shape, so he or she will not have to give up so much. This once again comes down to financial responsibility. That means the entrepreneur can't spend more than he or she has and must use the current resources to grow the business. I am working with two other guys and we have created a healthy tea called Ju'bilee Tea. We are using this "bootstrap" technique to get this company going. The next system we will discuss, most people have heard about it or personally encountered it in their life.

Stock Market System

The stock market is a manmade system full of flaws. The market is led by man's emotions. The retail investor always claims that the market is rigged against them like a casino in Las Vegas. There is some truth to this belief but probably not what you would expect me to say about gambling and the stock market. They are both manmade systems which mean that the casino and stock market is set up to benefit certain people. The odds are definitely against you when it comes to gambling. I feel as though you are just throwing money away. Of course some are able to overcome the odds with some skill and some luck but very few accomplish this goal. When they do win against the house, most people don't know when to quit and they give back all the money they just won. I have only gambled a few times because I know there are better places to put my resources. If I did win I would quit immediately.

It's all about discipline when it comes to managing finances. We have choices to make every day that get us closer to our goals or farther away. The choice is always ours to make. I will give you some of my own personal experiences in the stock market. I have bought and sold stocks, as well as, options in the stock market. I have bought and sold penny stocks, as well as stocks like Ford Motor Company. I will say there is a lot of manipulation with the penny stocks. People will do what I call the "pump n dump" on penny stocks. These guys are usually day traders. They are trying to make some quick money for the day. The day traders will pump up the price of a stock through news, volume or other speculative ways.

Once the day traders get enough people to buy into their plan the price increases and they sell their shares for a quick profit. In other words they "dump" the stock. If he doesn't realize what is going on, the retail investor can lose his money. I experienced this several times. I have become more aware of the day traders "pump n dump" plan. I have had both gains and losses. A manmade system is designed to benefit the party that created the system or the people who understand the system.

Real Estate System

Real estate market is another manmade system. I first experienced this system when I bought my first house. I bought a beautiful brand new house and I was so excited to be living in something so nice. I purchased the house for the amount the builder was asking for it. And of course the appraisal value was the same as the asking price. The bank had no problem loaning the money because all the numbers were to their satisfaction. As time went on the taxes got higher and the home values stayed the same. So I began to think about selling my house. This is when the manmade system really hit me. I was working seven days a week to pay the mortgage, taxes, insurance and all of my other bills. I began thinking: *who made the money on this house and who is paying for it?* Well, the builder, real estate agent and banker all made money but, I'm the one stuck working seven days a week to pay for it. This is a perfect example of a manmade system in everyday life. If you really think about it, it's like a bunch of systems working together. Now I will admit that when I bought the house, I was making more money so I could afford to live in the house. Once I was laid off, I couldn't find the same pay as before so I had to work two jobs. That doesn't change the system it just made it more obvious to me. So that meant that I had to sell the house and buy something that was in my new budget. Here is where most people will not get out of the manmade system.

The reason is very simple: everyone likes their new homes and doesn't want to give that up. Also no one likes to go backwards. I sold my house and bought a duplex in a lower income area. The best part was the other side was rented out so it paid my mortgage. Once I made this move, I gave myself a pay raise because I no longer had a big mortgage and tax payment, plus my new, lower mortgage was being paid from the rent I collected from the other side of the duplex.

You see I just flipped the real estate market (manmade system) around but in my favor. This was the beginning of my real estate investments which I will discuss in greater detail later on in the book. The point I'm trying to make is that there is a manmade system in real estate market that is designed to benefit certain people. No system should be allowed to represent the seller and buyer at the same time and tell me they have our best interest in mind. This system is definitely set up for the real estate industry to benefit the most from each transaction. My first and hardest lesson in real estate is to never ever pay retail. That is what the manmade system wants you to do. That's what keeps the system going if everyone pays retail for their homes. Now I believe everyone has a right to make money in real estate so I'm not implying these are bad people. They are just going with the system like everyone else. I'm not like everyone else. My wife and I have a house picked out and we will wait until it's the right time to buy it. That's not how the manmade system works; it's always saying buy now it won't last long, someone else will get it.

Multi-Level Marketing System

For some reason this manmade system is very popular in the Church. I am reminded of a company in my local area that would sell you a "travel agency" business based online. I remember people in my church signing up for this and paying the start-up fee and then a monthly rate for the website. *It's the greatest thing in the world*, is what people thought. I believed it was even started by a Pastor. Would you like to know where that business is today? It doesn't exist because there was no true business to begin with. Eventually you run out of people to sign up and you have no more growth. MLM and network marketing is the modern day pyramid selling technique.

They are emotionally driven by marketing the financial freedom, flexible work hours and all the other great benefits of owning your own business. My problem with MLM is that you don't actually own your own business. So for me they are deceiving everyone right up front. If someone else is making money off your work, then you are still working for someone else. When you own your own business you take all the risk and receive all the reward. The MLM system is setup to benefit the guys who set it up. The only people that really benefit are the ones on top of the pyramid. These people are very good marketers. And yes there are success stories, but very few compared to the failures. There is no easy get rich quick technique that you can use to get wealth. It requires hard work and time.

I recently went to a MLM seminar. Everything they talked about is the same rhetoric I have heard before. The numbers were a little confusing from level to level so I went to another meeting so I could get a better understanding of the numbers. This is what I discovered: the guys/gals at the top would get approximately $500,000 gross profit, if I signed up a certain amount of people. My take would be a measly $1500 a month residual income. Most people don't look at the amount they are making the people at the top. They just look at the potential numbers that they can earn. We need to have top-down thinking, instead of looking-up-to-the-top mentality.

CHAPTER 4
Kingdom System

Now I get to talk about the Kingdom system. This will be about personal experiences and examples from the Bible. The Bible is where we will find the principals for the Kingdom System. In the Kingdom System the basis is your heart. The world system is all about the individual. The world has a very selfish view. It has an all about "me" attitude. The Kingdom System is the complete opposite. It's about other people. That means that we think of other people before we think about ourselves. God's system is designed to be a giving system, not a taking system. He wants us to think about how we can **help** people, not what we can get **from** people. This makes our motives much different than the worlds. In order to live a life like this we must have God's heart. He has a heart of compassion. He also looks at the good in a person. The world likes to see the negative side of a person or situation. In the Kingdom System there is always a positive side to every situation or person. This comes from listening to our heart instead of listening to our emotions.

Emotions are not the same as compassion. Emotions are from the flesh. Compassion is from the heart. In Matthew 18:33 Jesus said "Should you not also have had compassion on your fellow servant, just as I had pity on you?" In 1 Peter 3:8 "Finally, all of you be of one mind, having compassion for one another; love as brothers, be tenderhearted, be courteous;" Also when Jesus had compassion for someone, He would heal them. In Matthew 9:35, 36 "Then Jesus went about all the cities and villages, teaching in their synagogues, preaching the gospel of the kingdom, and healing every sickness and every disease among the people. But when He saw the multitudes, He was moved with compassion for them, because they were weary and scattered, like sheep having no shepherd." Faith is a very important part of the Kingdom system. We must have faith in the Kingdom system even if we don't see things going our way.

God expects us to have faith in His system. The world systems require no faith in them because we can all see the results in the physical realm. In the Kingdom system we know the results but can't see them in the physical realm and do not know when it will come to pass. In 2 Corinthians 5:7 "For we walk by faith, not by sight."

Let me give you an example to help explain this point. I recently read an article about a town that went bankrupt in New England. Once this happened the city workers lost their pensions. Now see the world system says we pay union dues and the union will guarantee a retirement plan for us. There are no guarantees in this world system except death and taxes. If we will put our faith in the Kingdom system then God will provide for us. Even if the city, town, state, or country went bankrupt God will still provide for us. In Romans 5:1-5 "Therefore, having been justified by faith, we have peace with God through our Lord Jesus Christ, through whom also we have access by faith into this grace in which we stand, and rejoice in hope of the glory of God. And not only that, but we also glory in tribulations, knowing that tribulation produces perseverance; and perseverance, character; and character, hope. Now hope does not disappoint, because the love of God has been poured out in our hearts by the Holy Spirit who was given to us." It is much harder to have faith in the Kingdom system than the world system. The rewards are also much greater in the Kingdom system.

Success System

In the world system we wait until someone has success and then they write a book about their life, experiences, and successes. My Heavenly Father already considers me successful. The reason I know this is because He told me so. I am writing this book because I am successful in the spirit realm. It will manifest in the natural realm as soon as the natural realm catches up with the spiritual realm. This is all about God's timing. So what I am doing is writing this book as though my success has already manifested in the natural realm. This is a different way of thinking that does not happen in the world system.

CHAPTER 5
Wisdom

In Proverbs 4:7 "Wisdom is the principal thing; therefore get wisdom. And in all your getting, get understanding." Also in Proverbs 4:5 "Get wisdom! Get understanding! Do not turn away from the words of my mouth." Now the question is: who do we get our wisdom from? In Proverbs 4:1-4 "Hear my children, the instruction of a father, and give attention to know understanding; for I give you good doctrine: do not forsake my law. When I was my father's son, tender and the only one in the sight of my mother, He also taught me, and said to me: "Let your heart retain my words; keep my commands and live." This means that we get our wisdom from our natural father and our spiritual Father. When I have a question about something, I don't go to Facebook, I ask my Dad. He has more wisdom than me. Also my Heavenly Father knows everything, so He can help me the best. Therefore God is my source for wisdom. In Proverbs 9:10 "The fear of the Lord is the beginning of wisdom, and the knowledge of the Holy One is understanding." In Proverbs 9:9 "Give instruction to a wise man, and he will be still wiser; teach a just man, and he will increase in learning."

In James 1:5 "If any of you lack wisdom, let him ask God, who gives to all liberally and without reproach, and it will be given to him." In 1 Corinthians 3:18-20 "Let no one deceive himself. If anyone among you seems to be wise in this age, let him become a fool that he may become wise. For the wisdom of this world is foolishness with God. For it is written, "He catches the wise in their own craftiness"; and again, "The Lord knows the thoughts of the wise, that they are futile." In Ecclesiastes 12:9-14 "And moreover, because the Preacher was wise, he still taught the people knowledge; yes, he pondered and sought out and set in order many proverbs. The Preacher sought to find acceptable words; and what was written was upright-words of truth. The words of the wise are like goads, and the words of scholars are like well-driven nails, given by one Shepherd. And further, my son be admonished by these. Of making many books there is no end and much study is wearisome to the flesh. Let us hear the conclusion of the whole matter: Fear God and keep His commandments, for this is man's all. For God will bring every work into judgment, including every secret thing, whether good or evil." God is the ONE true source of wisdom, knowledge and understanding. The world is trying to get everyone to look to media, education systems, and religion for their wisdom. In John 8:32 Jesus said, "And you shall know the truth, and the truth shall make you free."

The problem is that so many people are bound by worldly systems that they cannot see the truth. We must trust in the one true source in order to break free from these systems. Micah 7:5a "Do not trust in a friend; do not put your confidence in a companion." Psalm 32:10 "Many sorrows shall be to the wicked; but he who trusts in the Lord, mercy shall surround him."   Proverbs 28:26 "He who trusts in his own heart is a fool, but whoever walks wisely will be delivered." Proverbs 3:5 "Trust in the Lord with all your heart, and lean not on your own understanding; in all your ways acknowledge Him, and He shall direct your paths."   Psalms 37:3 "Trust in the Lord, and do good; dwell in the land, and feed on His faithfulness." God gave us the book of wisdom. It's called the Bible. Our problem is we don't use what God gave us. The next principal is my favorite, which is sowing into the Kingdom System to reap a harvest.

CHAPTER 6
Sowing and Reaping

I enjoy sowing into the Kingdom. This is one of the many gifts God has given me. For some people it is very hard to sow, but once you start it becomes second nature. Sowing is just like eating food for me. I don't have to think about it. I actually get upset with myself when I forget my tithe/offering at home. I know that God looks at the heart, so I don't dwell on it. The Kingdom principal for sowing is very simple; we reap what we sow. This is what excites me most about this principal. That means the more I sow the more I reap. It also means that if I sow bad seeds that I will reap a bad harvest. Many people realize the bad harvest but can't seem to realize that a good harvest is just a good decision away. The world system is trying to see what it can acquire while the Kingdom system is trying to give things away. In the Kingdom system, in order for us to acquire possessions, we must first sow into someone else. Then God will give us a harvest.

The difficult part about this system is being patient and waiting for the harvest to come to us. In Hebrews 6:11-12 "And we desire that each one of you show the same diligence to the full assurance of hope until the end, that you do not become sluggish but imitate those who through faith and patience inherit the promises." We receive the harvest in God's time, not when we think we need or want something. I will give you several personal examples that hopefully will help explain this principal. I recently got married at the age of 41. I have been sowing into the Kingdom system for many years and patiently waiting for my wife. I did not think I would have to wait this long to get married but I can tell you it was definitely worth the wait. She is more than I could even have imagined on my own. You see, this happened in God's timing, not mine. It was God who put us together, not the world. I have reaped an amazing harvest in this area and it has just begun. Isaiah 32:20 "Blessed are you who sow beside all waters, who send out freely the feet of the ox and donkey."

We must be willing to freely sow in order to reap the blessings of our Heavenly Father. In Hosea 10:12 "Sow for yourselves righteousness; reap in mercy; break up your fallow ground for it is time to seek the Lord, till He comes and rains righteousness on you." This is a very clear understanding of the sowing and reaping principal. He is saying that if we will seek Him, and sow righteousness, then we will reap mercy and righteousness. The very important part to see in this verse is that we must seek the Lord, and in His timing, we will reap a harvest. A big problem with the world system is that we can't wait for God's timing, so we decide to take matters into our own hands. This is not how God designed the system. We are to be dependent on Him. That is what He wants us to do. The parable about the sower is a good example. In Matthew 13:19-23 "When anyone hears the word of the kingdom, and does not understand it, then the wicked one comes and snatches away what was sown in his heart. This is he who received seed by the wayside. But he who received the seed on stony places, this is he who hears the word and immediately he receives it with joy; yet he has no root in himself, but endures only for a while. For when tribulation or persecution arises because of the word, immediately he stumbles." Now he who received seed among the thorns is he, who hears the word, and the cares of this world and the deceitfulness of riches choke the word, and he becomes unfruitful. But he who received seed on the good ground is he who hears the word and understands it, who indeed bears fruit and produces: some hundred-fold, some sixty, some thirty." What Jesus is explaining to us in this parable is the importance of the ground where the seed is being sown. That ground He is referring to is us. We must be a fertile ground so when the seed is sown into us, fruitfulness will take place. This is no different than a farmer who is planting his seed in the field. His crops will not grow in unfertile ground. We are to receive the seed that is sown into our lives so we can in turn sow seed into another person's life. This is how God's principal of multiplication will happen. Let me give you a great example of this; I have fertile ground for God to deposit seed into my life. I am the ground and the seed is the words for the book I am writing. Once the book is published then I will be sowing into millions of lives. And the people who read the book, if they have fertile ground and will receive the "seed", the words in this book, then they will sow into other people's lives and on and on it goes. This is the principal of multiplication. We will all reap an incredible harvest. This is the Kingdom system, in action.

The most common response I get from people when I am teaching about sowing and reaping is the fact that they think they have nothing to sow. I had no idea what was inside of me until I began writing this book. God has planted so many seeds in me. Now I have the honor of taking those seeds and sowing them into other people's lives. God always gives seed to the sower. I have been sowing for many years into the Kingdom of God. Sowing can be done in many different ways. We can give offerings to ministries. We can pray for people. We can help people. We can give of our time or skill. There are many ways to sow into the Kingdom. Reaping what we sow is a Kingdom principal. We never know when the harvest will come from our sowing; we just know it will come.

This is a guarantee from Heaven. That is different than the world system because it wants something right away. In the Kingdom system, God will give you the harvest when He knows that you need it. That means we are living by faith and trusting in God that our harvest will come in His time. We give of ourselves to reap a harvest at a later time. This could come in an hour, a day, a week, a year or maybe even a decade or two from now. The world doesn't think like this at all. The world wants it now and doesn't care what it has to do to get it. The world will jeopardize their soul to get what they want out of life. The world is living in the moment and not thinking about any future consequences. In Galatians 6:6-10 "Let him who is taught the word share in all good things with him who teaches. Do not be deceived, God is not mocked; for whatever a man sows, that he will also reap. For he who sows to his flesh will of the flesh reap corruption, but he who sows to the Spirit will of the Spirit reap everlasting life. And let us not grow weary while doing good, for in due season we shall reap if we do not lose heart. Therefore, as we have opportunity, let us do good to all, especially to those who are of the household of faith."

In 2 Corinthians 6:6-10 "But this I say: He who sows sparingly will also reap sparingly, and he who sows bountifully will also reap bountifully. So let each one give as he purposes in his heart, not grudgingly or of necessity; for God loves a cheerful giver. And God is able to make all grace abound toward you, that you, always having all sufficiency in all things, may have an abundance for every good work. As it is written: He has dispersed abroad, He has given to the poor; His righteousness endures forever. Now may He who supplies seed to the sower, and bread for food, supply and multiply the seed you have sown and increase the fruits of your righteousness." This scripture describes the type of giver that God is looking for in the Kingdom system. We can give with a cheerful heart or a hard heart. God wants us to be a cheerful giver in His

Kingdom system. It says, "God loves a cheerful giver". God is looking at our heart when we give to His Kingdom. I remember a time when a prophet was coming to our area. I really wanted to give a big offering but I didn't have the resources to do so at the time. I gave what I could that weekend and I believe God saw my heart. God told me through my Pastor that He will make me exceedingly rich because of my support and heart of giving to the prophet. God looks at the heart of the giver, not the dollar amount. He always supplies resources to the people who will give into His Kingdom. God has all kinds of ways of getting our attention. The scriptures that I just wrote about have had a very unique impact on my life. One morning in church I was flipping through my Bible to get to a scripture my pastor was preaching about and I stopped at 2 Corinthians chapter 9. Now this was only the half of it. When I looked at the pages, I realized there was gold dust on the pages. So God was saying to me with a heavenly sign that this is real important. I've received other signs and wonders after this one, but I believe there is a reason He showed me my first sign on these pages. He is telling me how important it is to be a cheerful giver. I also believe He is telling me how pleased He is with my giving. These are just my personal interpretations of this sign. For more information on signs and wonders, read Bill Vincent's book: "Signs and Wonders."

When it comes to sowing and reaping, we have to remember that we are like farmers in a big field. We are the farmers and the world is the field. Every day we have opportunities to sow into the field. I would like to share with you two personal examples of sowing and reaping in real estate. I am always sowing into the Kingdom through offerings and helping people. I give to a missionary in our church that does ministry in Honduras. I also sell houses to Hispanic people. So I am giving into the Kingdom with the profits I receive from the houses I sell to Hispanics. There was a property that I looked at and the seller wanted $30,000. I thought that was too much so I didn't make any offer on it. Then maybe 6 months or so later, God spoke to me and said that I should drive by the property again. By this time, I had no interest in the property, but I drove by it anyway. The property was now listed with the realtor I used and the sign said "make offer". God spoke to me and said: "fifteen thousand" is the price to offer the seller. A few days later, I went to look at the property with my cousin and realtor. After we had inspected the property, I made the $15,000 offer. I told my realtor that was the only offer I was going to make. I would not go any higher. She said, ok and went to the seller's with the offer. My realtor called and told me after much discussion with the seller that they would agree to the price. The seller was not happy about the price but went through with it anyway. When God is the source of a business decision, it will always work out the way He planned it. I have made some decisions on my own and they did not turn out as well. God knows everything going on in the whole situation.

The reason I believe He blessed me with this property is because I have been sowing and also because I listened when He spoke to me. Obedience is very important. I will discuss that in another part of the book. I bought that property and then sold it to some Hispanic people and they are enjoying their own home. The second example I would like to discuss involves another property. My best friend's brother-in-law had a duplex that was going into foreclosure. I took a look at the property and it was not worth what he was trying to sell it for which was $90,000. So during prayer at church God spoke to me and said to offer $30,000. I offered the $30,000 and the bank which had the final say so because it was a short sale, came back with a counter offer of $90,000.

I thought: *well, I did what God had instructed me to do.* Many months go by and the brother-in-law says he deeded the property to the bank and they are going to auction it off online. I had completely forgotten about this property. Since the auction was three days away, I didn't have time to get a bank approval. So I signed up and was ready for the auction. I was working midnights and sleeping during the day when this auction was to take place. I had my dad take my place in the auction and just said, "I don't want to pay more than $30,000. So at the end of the auction I paid $31,500 for the property.

When I called my banker to let him know I had won the auction, he said, "What property? I didn't get the message". I was thinking: *oh boy, I just bought this property and I don't even have any kind of pre-approval!* God will always provide when He is in it. The banker was able to get the loan to go through and everything went according to God's plan. I am so thankful to my Heavenly and earthly father for everything they did for me that day. I fixed the property and rented it out to people and then when I got married in January of 2013, my wife and I are living in one side of it until we get our dream house.

I find it amazing that God knew I would need that property a year and a half later to live in with my wife. I would also like to say that just because it didn't happen right away doesn't mean that God miss spoke or I didn't hear Him correctly. God has His way of doing things that are way different than what we are able to understand. In Isaiah 55:8-9 "For My thoughts are not your thoughts, nor are your ways My ways, says the Lord. For as the heavens are higher than the earth, so are My ways higher than your ways, and My thoughts than your thoughts."

CHAPTER 7
Obedience and Favor

One of God's principals is obedience. Since the very beginning of creation, obedience has been a principal for His Kingdom. In the garden, Adam and Eve could eat of every tree except one. In Genesis 2:16-17 " And the Lord God commanded the man saying, "Of every tree of the garden you may freely eat; but of the tree of the knowledge of good and evil you shall not eat, for in the day that you eat of it you shall surely die." This shows us how important obedience is to our Heavenly Father. Obedience is hard for most of us. This principal is not easy to follow. Most people have trouble in this area. I have had years and years of disobedience. In fact, the writing of this book is an act of obedience. My Heavenly Father has wanted me to write this book for some time. I didn't want to write a book because I'm not naturally creative. I am also not a writer. The Holy Spirit is helping me write this book. Writing this book is not easy for me. When I sit down the Holy Spirit gives me the words to put in the book. I can tell you that this is not my book. I have to trust in Him. In Psalms 71:5 "For You are my hope, O Lord God; You are my trust from my youth." He is my source for this book.

We must obey and trust in Him. Our Heavenly Father wants us to look up to Him for guidance. When we do trust in Him we will receive the favor of God. This favor includes the favor of man. In Deuteronomy 11:26,27a "Behold, I set before you today a blessing and a curse: "the blessing, if you obey the commandments of the Lord your God which I command you today". In 1 Samuel 15:21-22 "But the people took of the plunder, sheep and oxen, the best of the things which should have been utterly destroyed, to sacrifice to the Lord your God in Gilgal. So Samuel said: Has the Lord great delight in burnt offerings and sacrifices, as in obeying the voice of Lord? Behold, to obey is better than sacrifice, and to heed than the fat of rams". Saul went on a mission for the Lord and didn't obey the words of the Lord. He told Saul to destroy all of the Amalekites and the spoil. Saul chose to save the best spoil and sacrifice it to God.

This is not the instruction that Saul received from the Prophet Samuel. Saul was doing what he thought was best, instead of obeying God's instructions. I believe we have all been like Saul at some time in our lives. I know that I did not obey God all of the time. We have to learn from these mistakes. God gives us instructions for a reason. He is our heavenly Father and He does know what is best for us. Also He wants to give us more, but we have to be trusted at our current level. Saul had an opportunity to go even higher in the Kingdom of God. When he disobeyed God and took matters into his own hand, God rejected him from being king. So you see Saul lost his favor with God and man. As I mentioned earlier, I have procrastinated on writing this book. I received several prophetic words from different prophets about writing books. I believed it was for later on in life. I also believed that I had to be successful to write this book. I just needed to be obedient to God's instructions. I believe when this book is finished that my wife and I will have the favor of God and man. God knows the next season of our lives and He is trying to get us there. We need to be obedient and carry out the instructions He has given us, so we can get to the next level in our lives. In Isaiah 1:19-20 "If you are willing and obedient, you shall eat the good of the land; but if you refuse and rebel, you shall be devoured by the sword; for the mouth of the Lord has spoken."

CHAPTER 8
Giving and Receiving

I would like to tell you my personal experience with giving and receiving. I am a natural giver. I enjoy giving to people. My problem was the receiving part. I had a hard time receiving from people. I felt that I should always be giving to other people. I remember when someone came up to me and gave me $100. That meant a lot to me because I was not working at the time. This is when God set me free from the religious mind set of giving and not receiving. I had prophesied to the person who gave me the money. So you see, I gave to him and he received it. Now he was giving to me and I needed to receive it. God wants to give to us. I realized that the receiving was part of giving. Now if someone wants to give me something for no reason at all, I know it's because I gave to someone else. The great part about the Kingdom system is that we cannot out-give God. That means we will receive more than we can give. In Malachi 3:10 "Bring all the tithes into the storehouse, that there may be food in My house, and try Me now in this says the Lord of hosts, if I will not open for you the windows of heaven and pour out for you such blessing that there will not be room enough to receive it." It's very important to be able to do both equally well. I actually expect to receive when I give into the Kingdom system. This is using the Kingdom principal in the manner God wanted it to be used. When we give, we should expect to receive. Why? Because God's principals work. He is perfect. Therefore any principal He made works in the same manner. Psalms 24:5 "He shall receive blessing from the Lord, and righteousness from the God of his salvation". John 16:24 "Until now you have asked nothing in my name. Ask, and you will receive, that your joy may be full".

Matthew 21:22 "And whatever things you ask in prayer, believing, you will receive".

CHAPTER 9
Forgiving and Loving

The world would want us to get revenge on someone that has hurt us. Just look at all the movies that are produced with revenge as the storyline. The world is full of hurting people. The Kingdom principal of forgiving and loving people that have hurt you is difficult for most people to understand. Everyone has had someone hurt them. It is so hard for us to forgive that person. And it is even more difficult to love that person. The best example of forgiving and loving people is our Lord and Savior, Jesus Christ and our Heavenly Father. First, our Heavenly Father sent His son to die for our sins. In John 3:16-17 "For God so loved the world that He gave His only begotten Son, that whoever believes in Him should not perish but have everlasting life." For God did not send His son into the world to condemn the world, but that the world through Him might be saved." And second, Jesus forgave the people who killed Him. In

Luke 23:34 "Then Jesus said, "Father, forgive them, for they do not know what they do."

We must follow Jesus example of forgiving. Colossians 3:13 "bearing with one another , and forgiving one another, if anyone has a complaint against another; even as Christ forgave you, so you also must do." We have to learn to love everyone. In John 15:9-10, 11-12 "As the Father loved Me, I also have loved you; abide in my love. If you keep My commandments, you will abide in My love, just as I have kept My Father's commandments and abide in His love. This is My commandment, that you love one another as I have loved you. Greater love has no one than this, than to lay down one's life for his friends." This includes our enemies. Luke 6:27-28 "But I say to you who hear: Love your enemies, do good to those who hate you, bless those who curse you, and pray for those who spitefully use you."

Proverbs 25:21 "If your enemy is hungry, give him bread to eat; and if he is thirsty, give him water to drink;" 1 John 4:7 "Beloved, let us love one another, for love is of God; and everyone who loves is born of God and knows God." We can't do this on our own strength. That is why our source of forgiveness and love has to come from God. Romans 5:5 "Now hope does not disappoint, because the love of God has been poured out in our hearts by the Holy Spirit who was given to us."

CHAPTER 10
Choices

Now I know that every person lives in one or more of these world systems. We can still use the Kingdom system within the world system. In Romans 12:2 "And do not be conformed to this world, but be transformed by the renewing of your mind, that you may prove what is that good and acceptable and perfect will of God." Each day we have opportunities to make choices. Some choices are good and some are bad. We have to remember that the choices we make influence the direction that we will go. The world system, as a whole, doesn't think about the future. The Kingdom system is always looking at the future. This is our responsibility. No one can do this for us. This is a process. It requires time, faith, and patience. Choosing the Kingdom system over the world's system does make life a lot harder in the beginning. As you start to see the goodness of the Kingdom system at work you will be glad you made the choice. This is how we bring Heaven to earth. Instead of us trying to get to Heaven, we can have Heaven on earth if we will follow the Kingdom principals. God expects us to make choices and be responsible for those choices. Society is always trying to push the blame to someone else. Our God is a great and loving God. We do make choices that open us up to bad things. Some people want to blame God for this but we made the choice not God. Romans 8:28 "And we know that all things work together for good to those who love God, to those who are the called according to His purpose." In order for us to fully understand the Kingdom system we will need to die to ourselves and live life by the Kingdom principals. We cannot do this on our own.

The only way is to have God inside of us. In Galatians 2:19 "For I through the law died to the law that I might live to God." Also in Galatians 5:24 "And those who are Christ's have crucified the flesh with its passions and desires." I have chosen the Kingdom system over the world system. So God is my source. So the question is: who is your $ource?

Contact the Author

Kevin Cann

Kingdom Management & Investments, LLC

Email:
kevincann@kingdommanagement101.com

Website: kingdommanagment101.com

Recommended Book

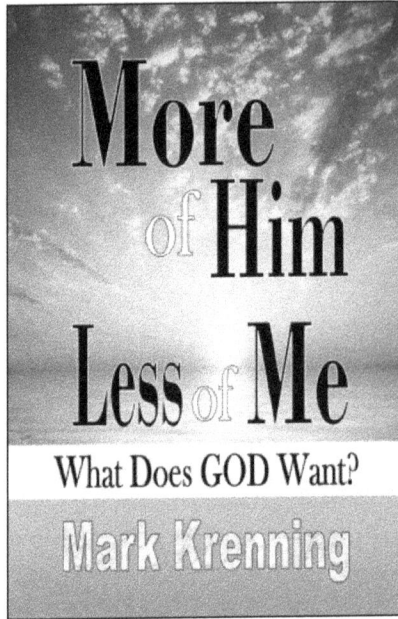

God ways are not our ways and HIS thoughts are not our thoughts. More of HIM.... Less of Me explains how God has revealed himself to me. How HE has used what was meant for my destruction to bring me closer to HIM and how HE has given me a deeper revelation of what was accomplished through Jesus' life, death, and resurrection.

Available anywhere books are sold.